ARACHNID WORLD

TARANTULAS

SANDRA MARKLE

WITHDRAWN

SUPERSIZED PREDATORS

LERNER PUBLICATIONS COMPANY MINNEAPOLIS

FOR CURIOUS KIDS EVERYWHERE

ACKNOWLEDGMENTS
The author would like to thank Rick C. West, American Tarantula Society and past honorary
research associate with the Royal British Columbia Museum, Victoria, British Columbia,
Canada; and Dr. Simon Pollard, Canterbury Museum, Christchurch, New Zealand, for
sharing their expertise and enthusiasm. A special thanks to Skip Jeffery for his support
during the creation of this book.

Lerner Publications Company
A division of Lerner Publishing Group, Inc.
241 First Avenue North
Minneapolis, MN 55401 U.S.A.

Website address: www.lernerbooks.com

Library of Congress Cataloging-in-Publication Data

Markle, Sandra.
    Tarantulas : supersized predators / by Sandra Markle.
        p.   cm. — (Arachnid world)
    Includes bibliographical references and index.
    ISBN 978–0–7613–5043–9 (lib. bdg. : alk. paper)
    1. Tarantulas—Juvenile literature. I. Title.
    QL458.42.T5M35 2012
    595.4'4—dc23   2011020437

Manufactured in the United States of America
1 - DP - 12/31/11

CONTENTS

AN ARACHNID'S WORLD

WELCOME TO THE WORLD OF ARACHNIDS

(ah-RACK-nidz). Arachnids can be found in every habitat on Earth except in the deep ocean. Some are even found in Antarctica.

So how can you tell if an animal is an arachnid rather than a relative like the insect shown below? Both arachnids and insects belong to a group of animals called arthropods (AR-throh-podz). All animals in this group share some traits.

They have bodies divided into segments, jointed legs, and a stiff exoskeleton. This is a skeleton on the outside like a suit of armor. But one way to tell if an animal is an arachnid is to count its legs and body parts. While not every adult arachnid has eight legs, most do. Arachnids also usually have two main body parts. Giant wetas, like the one above, are as big as the largest spiders, but they are insects. They have six legs and three main body parts.

This book is about one special family of arachnids—tarantulas. Tarantulas are spiders. Like all spiders, they're predators and must catch and kill other animals to live. Many kinds of tarantulas, like this Brazilian pinktoe tarantula *(facing page)*, are the biggest spiders. They're supersized hunters.

TARANTULA FACT

A tarantula's body temperature rises and falls with the temperature around it. It must warm up to be active.

So how big are the largest tarantulas? The pinkfoot goliath tarantulas, like this female, are among the world's largest. The distance between its outstretched legs is about 11 inches (28 centimeters), or about as big as a dinner plate. Being big is an advantage. It lets a tarantula hunt and catch prey too big for most spiders to safely tackle. This female pinkfoot goliath tarantula was able to catch and kill a nearly 2-foot-long (0.5-meter) fer-de-lance snake.

TARANTULA FACT

The smallest kind of tarantula is the Paloma dwarf. Males, which are a little smaller than females, have a leg span of about 1 inch (2.5 cm). That's still larger than many kinds of spiders.

When threatened, a tarantula lifts up the front end of its body *(below)*. This defensive pose makes it look even bigger. It also displays its fangs.

A tarantula's fangs fold back like a pocketknife when not in use. As the spider prepares to strike, the fangs move downward and outward. Each fang has a tiny opening near the end. When the tarantula stabs its prey—or an enemy—it injects liquid poison called venom through an opening in each fang. A tarantula's venom isn't as powerful as the venom of some smaller spiders, like a black widow. But because of its size, a tarantula can deliver more venom than most other spiders do. It's enough to kill large prey.

TARANTULA FACT

A tarantula's venom isn't usually strong enough to kill humans. For most people, its effect is about the same as a beesting. A few people, though, can have a serious allergic reaction.

FANG

Tarantulas aren't just big. They're also hairy. Many of their hairs, called setae, are special sensors. These let the tarantula detect air movement and heat. Some hairs near the tarantula's mouth sense chemicals. These let the tarantula taste what the hairs touch, like the frog in the picture.

PERUVIAN PINKTOE TARANTULA

Most tarantulas that live in North America, Central America, or South America have other special barbed hairs. These are on the top, rear, and sides of their abdomens. These hairs are very loosely attached to the tarantula's exoskeleton. When it needs to defend itself, a tarantula rubs its hind legs over its body to flick off these barbed hairs. The hairs cause pain and itching when they strike eyes or skin. That's enough to make most predators back off.

BARBED HAIRS

OUTSIDE AND INSIDE

ON THE OUTSIDE

There are about nine hundred different kinds of tarantulas. They all share certain features. They have two main body parts: the cephalothorax (sef-uh-loh-THOR-ax) and the abdomen. A waistlike part called the pedicel joins the two. The tarantula's exoskeleton is made up of many plates. Stretchy tissues connect the plates so the spider can bend and move.

Take a close look at the outside of this brown baboon tarantula to discover other key features tarantulas share.

ABDOMEN

SPINNERETS: These nozzlelike parts spin spider silk.

CLAWS: They are used for grabbing and hanging on. Unlike other spiders, the tarantula's claws, like a cat's claws, can be pulled back. Around the claws is a special cluster of hairs. These spread out and help the tarantula climb smooth surfaces and walk on water.

LEGS: These are used for walking and climbing.

PEDICEL

CEPHALOTHORAX

EYES:
These organs detect light and send messages to the brain for sight. Tarantulas have eight eyes arranged in two rows of four. Their eyes may only be able to tell light from dark.

PEDIPALPS:
These are a pair of leglike parts that extend from the head near the mouth. They help catch prey and hold it for eating. Males use the pedipalps during mating.

CHELICERAE
(keh-LISS-ee-ray):
This pair of jawlike parts is near the mouth and ends in fangs. The fangs are used to stab prey and inject venom.

ON THE INSIDE

Look inside an adult
female tarantula.

VENOM GLAND:
This body part
produces
venom.

BRAIN:
This part sends
and receives
messages to
and from body
parts.

**PHARYNX
(FAR-inks):**
This muscular tube
pumps food into the
stomach. Hairs in the
tube help filter out
solid waste.

**CAECA
(SEE-kuh):**
These branching
tubes pass food
nutrients into the
blood. They also
store food.

**COXAL
(KAHK-sel)
GLANDS:** These
special groups of cells
collect liquid wastes
and pass them through
openings to the
outside.

**NERVE
GANGLIA:**
These bundles
of nerve tissue send
messages between
the brain and other
body parts.

Approved by Dr. Simon
Pollard, Canterbury Museum,
Christchurch, New Zealand

SUCKING STOMACH: This stomach works with the pharynx to move food between the mouth and the gut. Cells in the lining produce digestive fluids.

HEART: This muscular tube pumps blood toward the head. Then the blood flows back to the heart.

MALPIGHIAN (mal-PIG-ee-an) TUBULES: This system of tubes cleans the blood of wastes.

GUT: This tube lets food nutrients pass into the blood.

STERCORAL (STER-kor-ul) POCKET: This is the place where wastes collect before passing out of the body.

OVARY: This body part produces eggs.

SILK GLAND: This body part produces silk.

BOOK LUNGS: These are thin, flat folds of tissue. Oxygen from the air passes through them and enters the spider's blood. Waste carbon dioxide gas exits.

GONOPORE: This is the reproductive opening.

SPERMATHECA (spur-muh-THEE-kuh): This sac stores sperm after mating.

BECOMING ADULTS

Like all arachnids, tarantulas go through incomplete metamorphosis. *Metamorphosis* means "change." In its lifetime, a tarantula goes through three main stages: egg, spiderling, and adult.

Compare this newly hatched Texas brown tarantula with its mother. It has lots of brothers and sisters that look just like it. The female laid nearly one thousand eggs in a saclike web. Then she stayed on guard for almost two months until they hatched. Although the baby is much smaller, it has many of the adult's features. The spiderling will hunt, eat, and behave much like the adult. It will be nearly ten years before this kind of tarantula becomes an adult, ready to mate and produce young.

SOME ARTHROPODS GO THROUGH COMPLETE METAMORPHOSIS. The stages are egg, larva, pupa, and adult. Each stage looks and behaves very differently.

SPIDERLING

15

Most tarantula spiderlings stay in their mother's burrow for about two weeks after they hatch. During this time, they continue to develop and molt (shed their exoskeleton). Just by being with their mother, they're protected from bigger predators, such as lizards. Some female tarantulas also bring up some liquid digested food from their stomachs. This provides the spiderlings with their first meal.

Peruvian chicken tarantula spiderlings *(facing page)* stay with their mother for almost a year. Besides keeping them safe, their mother sometimes catches food for them. When she killed a tree frog (yellow), the young tarantulas rushed to compete for a share of this meal.

TREE FROG

MOLTING TO GROW

While a tarantula grows bigger, a new exoskeleton forms underneath the old one. Many kinds of spiders molt by hanging from a silk strand while they pull their legs and body out of their old exoskeleton. A tarantula is too heavy to molt that way. It spins a silk mat on the ground and molts on this. As this Ecuadorian brown velvet tarantula starts to molt, it flips over onto its back on its mat. The old exoskeleton splits open. Then the tarantula tugs out its body and legs.

TARANTULA FACT

Tarantula spiderlings usually molt several times a year for as much as ten years, until they become adults. Most spiders don't molt as adults. But female adult tarantulas molt about once a year.

When a tarantula molts, something amazing can happen. It can regenerate, or develop a replacement for, a lost part, such as a leg. This Salt Lake City brown tarantula has one leg that's thinner and lighter than the others. That's because it's been regenerated. Regeneration only happens if the body part is lost through an injury at the beginning of a growth period. The replacement develops folded up inside the old exoskeleton. The new part unfolds the next time the tarantula molts. The regenerated part may be a little shorter or thinner. But it will work just like the original.

TARANTULA FACT

Sometimes, while catching prey or fighting off predators, fangs and spinnerets are lost or damaged. Tarantulas that are still growing may also regenerate those parts.

A SPINNING LIFE

Like all spiders, tarantulas spin silk. The silk comes out of the nozzlelike spinnerets *(below)*. The silk starts out as a gooey liquid. It becomes a solid strand when the tarantula fastens it to something—even to its own leg—and pulls.

TARANTULA FACT

Unlike other spiders, tarantulas also squirt out silk from their feet. They do this to help them hold on when moving across a slick surface.

Tarantulas don't use their silk to build web traps to catch prey, as many spiders do. Most hunt prey by waiting and pouncing. Sometimes, they wander to hunt. Then they may spin a silk strand to trail behind them. They anchor this, from time to time, with sticky silk. If they fall, this line gives them a tether to help them drop safely to the ground. But tarantulas are too heavy to dangle from their silk lines. So as it climbs down, this Mexican red rump tarantula *(below)* also holds on tight with its claw-tipped feet.

Some tarantulas live in burrows. Their home may be a natural hole in a tree or the ground or another animal's abandoned burrow. Some tarantulas, like this Mexican redleg tarantula, use their fangs and feet to dig a burrow. Once a tarantula moves into its home, it's likely to spin silk at the entrance. Then the spider sits in its home with its feet touching the silk strands. These strands let the tarantula sense movement close by. If the tarantula senses strong movements, it pulls back into its burrow and hides. A bigger predator could be close. If it senses weaker movements, prey could be close. Then the tarantula charges to attack.

Some tarantulas hunt high up in trees instead of on the ground. This pinktoe tarantula lives in the rain forest. It spins silk to create a pocketlike shelter high up on a tree. The shelter's opening faces down. That way, heavy rains won't flood its home. Like ground-dwelling tarantulas, it sits and waits to ambush prey.

Female tarantulas spin silk for another reason. They use their silk to form a sac for their eggs. This female Mexican redknee tarantula spun a hanging silk mat. On it she deposits several hundred eggs.

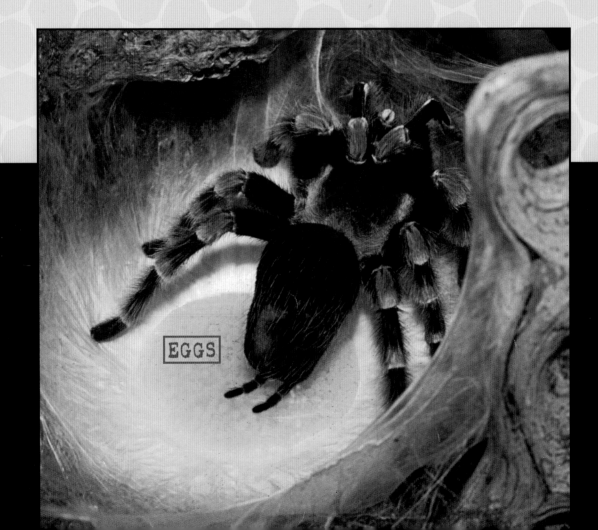

EGGS

Then she spins more silk to cover her eggs. She rolls up the silk and eggs to create a sturdy egg sac. The female guards the egg sac in her burrow for nearly two months as the young develop. If she moves to a new burrow, she uses her chelicerae and pedipalps to carry her egg sac with her.

TARANTULA FACT

Some tarantulas also stick some of their defensive hairs onto their silk egg sac. This keeps flies from laying their eggs on the sac. If the fly eggs hatched on the sac, the fly's larvae (young) would chew into it. Then the larvae would grow up eating the tarantula's eggs and young.

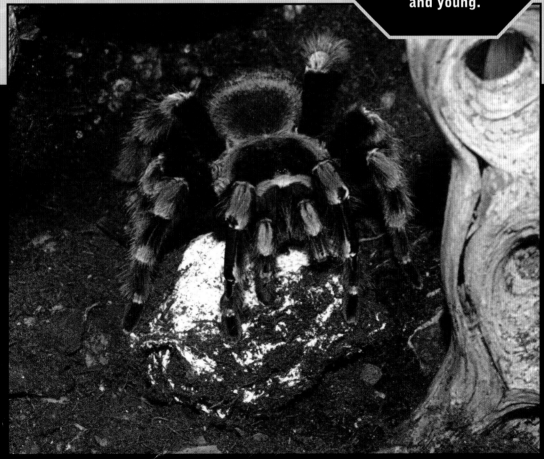

A GOLIATH'S STORY

Shadows lengthen and blend together as day becomes night in the Amazon rain forest in Brazil. The air cools slightly but is no less damp and humid. Brilliantly colored birds and noisy monkeys settle in the trees for the night. Down on the forest floor, though, a female goliath bird-eater tarantula spiderling is hunting. She sits and waits until a gecko comes close. Then she pounces on her prey. She is new at hunting. Until a few days ago, she lived with more than fifty brothers and sisters in their mother's burrow. Being with their mother, the spiderlings stayed safe. However, their mother didn't supply any food, so the spiderlings had to leave the burrow to hunt for themselves. A gecko will give this spiderling the energy she needs to keep on hunting and to grow bigger.

TARANTULA FACT

Bigger tarantulas will catch and eat smaller ones—even their own brothers or sisters.

With a leg span of over 1 inch (3 cm), the goliath bird-eater tarantula spiderling is already about the size of a quarter. She's big enough to easily kill prey as big as she is. That's prey bigger than most other kinds of spiderlings can safely catch.

She has fewer enemies than most spiderlings because she's too big for smaller predators to kill. However, she's still in danger of becoming a meal for bigger predators. When a snake slithers close, the spiderling lifts the front half of her body to look bigger than she is.

When the snake comes still closer, the spiderling turns her back on her enemy. She quickly rubs her abdomen with her back leg. This launches lots of barbed hairs toward the snake. It slides away, and the spiderling escapes.

Being a nighttime hunter, the goliath bird-eater tarantula spiderling spends her days in her burrow. At night, she most often hunts by sitting in her burrow entrance. If her sensitive hairs pick up strong air movement, she backs up to hide. Tonight, though, she senses weak movements. The spiderling charges out and stabs an earthworm with her fangs. The venom she injects from her fangs quickly kills the earthworm.

The spiderling tugs her prey into her burrow to eat. Digestive juices injected with her venom are already breaking down the earthworm's soft tissue. Next, the spiderling folds back her fangs. This crushes part of the earthworm against the rows of sharp teeth edging each chelicera. The spiderling also brings up more digestive juices. The mashed part of the earthworm changes into a gooey liquid that the spiderling sucks in. Then she repeats this process until she's eaten the whole worm.

TARANTULA FACT

Some tarantulas carry their waste pellets out of their burrow. Others have a special chamber in their burrow where they deposit garbage. Either way, this keeps the wastes from attracting other predators, such as lizards and snakes, that might attack them.

Over the next two weeks, the goliath bird-eater tarantula spiderling eats and grows bigger. Soon her body is so big her exoskeleton becomes tight. A new exoskeleton has already developed underneath the old one, and she molts. Her new exoskeleton is soft at first. So she forces blood into different parts of her body to stretch her soft exoskeleton. This way, like wearing clothes that are too big, the spiderling has room to grow before she has to molt yet again.

As a tarantula gets ready to molt, its body produces special fluids that help separate it from its old exoskeleton. Once the exoskeleton breaks open, a tarantula works hard to pull its body free.

The spiderling wanders in search of another burrow where she can hide. And she keeps on hunting and growing.

OLD EXOSKELETON

THE CYCLE CONTINUES

By the time the goliath bird-eater tarantula is five years old, she's an adult. (Other kinds of tarantulas may take longer to become adults.)

An adult female goliath bird-eater has a nearly 1-foot-wide (30 cm) leg span and weighs about 6 ounces (170 grams). She moves into an even bigger burrow. She spins her silk patio in front of the entrance. Then she sits on this with her feet touching the silk strands to feel when a predator or a prey animal is close.

Even bigger prey, such as big frogs and mice, are fair game for her now. Such big meals give her an energy boost and extra nutrients. She needs this food because her body is preparing to produce eggs. Once she's ready to mate, the silk strands she spins are coated with pheromones, or special chemicals. These chemicals signal that she's a goliath bird-eater tarantula female seeking a mate. A male goliath bird-eater tarantula tracks the pheromones to find her.

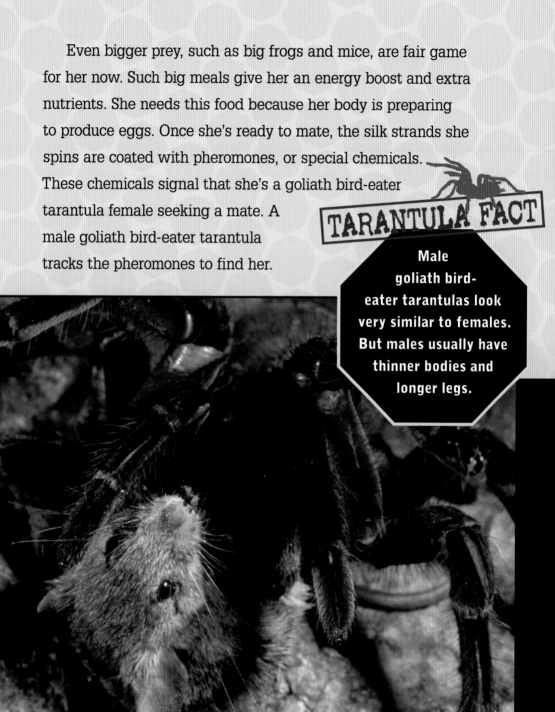

TARANTULA FACT

Male goliath bird-eater tarantulas look very similar to females. But males usually have thinner bodies and longer legs.

When he reaches the female's burrow entrance, the male drums the ground with his pedipalps. He also shakes his abdomen. These vibrations (movements) draw out the female. The pair face off and fence with their legs. He pushes her upright. The male inserts the sperm he's carrying in his pedipalps into the female's gonopore. Then he leaves.

The female continues to hunt big prey to gain enough energy for her eggs to develop. Once they're ready to be deposited, she spins a silk mat and deposits about fifty pea-sized eggs on it. She covers the eggs with more silk and rolls it into an egg sac. She'll guard this sac for nearly two months while her young develop. These will be her first offspring, but she'll have more. The female goliath bird-eater tarantula may live fourteen years or even longer. As long as she can hunt successfully and avoid predators, she'll mate every year or two. With each brood, the goliath bird-eater tarantula's cycle of life continues.

TARANTULA FACT

A female tarantula may need to eat for nearly a year before she gains enough energy for her eggs to develop. If she doesn't find enough to eat, her eggs may never develop.

TARANTULAS AND OTHER BIG ARACHNIDS

TARANTULAS belong to a group, or order, of arachnids called Araneae (ah-RAN-ee-ay). This order contains the spider members of the arachnid group. Tarantulas belong to a family of spiders, the Theraphosidae (ther-ah-FAH-seh-die). There are over nine hundred different kinds worldwide. They can be found on every continent except Antarctica.

SCIENTISTS GROUP living and extinct animals with others that are similar. So tarantulas are classified this way:

kingdom: Animalia
phylum: Arthropoda
class: Arachnida
order: Araneae
family: Theraphosidae

HELPFUL OR HARMFUL? Tarantulas are mainly helpful. They eat a lot of insects. This way they help control insects that could otherwise become pests. Tarantulas only bite people in self-defense. Like all spiders, tarantulas inject venom when they bite. Their venom is weak, but some people may have an allergic reaction to it.

HOW BIG IS a goliath bird-eater tarantula female? Its body length is about 5 inches (13 cm). Its leg span is about 12 inches (30 cm).

MORE BIG ARACHNIDS

A tarantula's big size helps it catch food and stay safe. Check out how being big helps each of these arachnids.

Emperor scorpions are the biggest scorpions in the world. Adults can reach about 8 inches (20 cm) in length. These African natives are massive, the tanks of the arachnid world. They're also armed with both powerful pincers and a stinger. However, emperor scorpions mainly eat small termites. Empire scorpions depend on their size and built-in weapons for defense against reptiles and mammals. Their babies, called scorplings, are born unable to defend themselves. They ride on their mother's back and count on her defenses until they are ready to take care of themselves.

Giant golden orb web spiders are the biggest of the orb weaver spiders. Actually only the females are big. They may have a leg span of about 4 inches (10 cm). By comparison, the males are tiny, averaging one-fifth the female's size. Found in Africa, female giant golden orb web spiders build the world's biggest webs—often more than 3 feet (1 meter) across. With these big webs, they are able to catch flying insects too big for other web weavers to trap. Unlike most spiders, a group of golden orb web spiders will hook their webs together. That builds super traps that can be as much as 200 feet (61 m) tall.

GLOSSARY

abdomen: the rear end of an arachnid. It contains systems for digestion, reproduction and, in spiders, silk production.

adult: the reproductive stage of an arachnid's life cycle

book lungs: thin flat folds of tissue where blood circulates. Air enters through slits and passes between these tissue folds, allowing oxygen to enter the blood. Waste carbon dioxide gas exits through them.

brain: the organ that receives messages from the rest of the body and sends signals to control all body parts

caeca: branching tubes through which liquid food passes and where food is stored. Food nutrients pass from this tube into the blood and are carried throughout the body.

cephalothorax: the front end of an arachnid. It includes the mouth, the brain, and the eyes, if there are any. Legs are also attached to this part.

chelicerae: a pair of strong, jawlike parts that extend from the head in front of the mouth. In tarantulas they are edged in teeth to crush and tear. They end in fangs that can inject venom.

coxal gland: a special group of cells for collecting and getting rid of liquid wastes through openings to the outside of the body. They aid in maintaining water balance in the body.

egg: a female reproductive cell; also the name given to the first stage of an arachnid's life cycle

exoskeleton: a protective, armorlike covering on the outside of the body

eyes: sensory organs that detect light and send signals to the brain for sight

fangs: a pair of toothlike parts at the tip of the spider's chelicerae. Venom flows out of each fang through a hole near the tip.

heart: the muscular tube that pumps blood forward. Then the blood flows throughout the body and back to the heart.

Malpighian tubules: a system of tubes that cleans the blood of wastes and dumps them into the intestine

molt: the process of an arachnid shedding its exoskeleton

nerve ganglia: bundles of nerve tissue that send messages between the brain and other body parts

ovary: the body part that produces eggs

pedicel: the waistlike part in spiders that connects the cephalothorax to the abdomen

pedipalps: a pair of leglike body parts that extend from the head near the mouth. Pedipalps help catch prey and hold it for eating. In males the pedipalps are also used during reproduction.

pharynx: a muscular body part that contracts to create a pumping force, drawing food into the digestive system. Hairs filter out bits of solid waste.

pheromones: chemicals given off as a form of communication

regenerate: to regrow a lost body part

silk gland: the body part that produces silk

sperm: a male reproductive cell

spermatheca: the sac in female arachnids that stores sperm after mating

spiderling: the name given to the stage between egg and adult in spiders

spinneret: the body part that spins silk

stercoral pocket: a place where wastes collect before passing out of the body

sucking stomach: a muscular body part that works with the pharynx to pull liquid food into the arachnid's gut. Cells in the lining produce digestive juices.

venom: liquid poison

venom gland: the body part that produces venom

DIGGING DEEPER

To keep on investigating tarantulas and other spiders, explore these books and online sites.

BOOKS

Goldish, Meish. *Goliath Bird-Eating Tarantula: The World's Biggest Spider.* New York: Bearport Publishing, 2007. Take a close look at the life and behavior of the biggest kind of tarantula.

Gordon, David George. *Uncover a Tarantula: Take a Three-Dimensional Look Inside a Tarantula.* San Diego: Silver Dolphin Books, 2004. Assemble a model while exploring a tarantula's body. Also, investigate more about tarantula behavior.

Montgomery, Sy. *The Tarantula Scientist.* New York: Houghton Mifflin Books for Children, 2004. Follow tarantula scientist Sam Marshall at work in his lab and in the rain forests of French Guiana. Nic Bishop's amazing photographs bring the scientist and his subjects to life.

Silverstein, Alvin, Virginia Silverstein, and Laura Silverstein Nunn. *Creepy Crawlies.* Minneapolis: Lerner Publications Company, 2003. Discover which arachnids and insects make good pets and which ones don't.

Singer, Marilyn. *Venom.* Minneapolis: Millbrook Press, 2007. Find out about creatures that can harm or even kill with a bite or a sting.

Souza, D. M. *Packed with Poison!* Minneapolis: Millbrook Press, 2006. Learn about the most venomous and poisonous animals in the world.

MORE FROM SANDRA MARKLE

ARACHNID WORLD:
Black Widows
Harvestmen
Orb Weavers
Scorpions
Ticks
Wolf Spiders

WEBSITES

Desert USA: Tarantula

http://www.desertusa.com/july96/du_taran.html

Explore lots of facts about tarantulas. Don't miss clicking on the "more pictures of tarantulas" and video links.

Giantspiders.com

http://giantspiders.com/galleryhome.html

Go straight to the video link to investigate tarantulas up close and in action. Don't miss the microscopic views of tarantula body parts.

National Geographic: Tarantulas

http://video.nationalgeographic. com/video/player/animals/bugs- animals/spiders-and-scorpions/ tarantula_goliath.html

Don't miss this close-up look of a goliath tarantula hunting and killing prey.

LERNER SOURCE™

Visit www.lerneresource.com for free, downloadable arachnid diagrams, research assignments to use with this series, and additional information about arachnid scientific names.

TARANTULA ACTIVITY

This Para Mongo zebra tarantula has a leg span of about 8 inches (20 cm). It caught a frog about half that big. That was much bigger prey than most spiders can safely tackle. Like all tarantulas, it grew to its full size in stages. At each stage, it molted. Follow these steps to get a feel for why the tarantula molts. You'll also discover how the molting process happens.

1. Work with an adult partner to blow up a balloon. Only blow it up enough to slightly expand it. Tie the neck to seal the balloon.

2. Cover the balloon with papier-mâché. To do this, first snip a newspaper into strips about 1 inch (2.5 cm) wide and 6 inches (25 cm) long. Cut at least 25 strips. In a bowl, mix ½ cup flour with enough water to make a runny paste. Dip one paper strip into the paste mixture. Hold the strip over the bowl, and slide the strip between your thumb and fingers to remove excess paste. Smooth the strip onto the balloon. Repeat until the whole balloon is covered up to the neck. Smooth your fingers over the wet balloon. This will help seal the edges of the paper strips. Set the balloon in a clean, dry bowl. Turn every few hours to help it dry evenly. Leave overnight.

3. The balloon now represents your tarantula spiderling. Use scissors to carefully snip into the balloon just below the knotted neck. The balloon will deflate and separate from the inside of the papier-mâché.

4. Carefully pull the deflated balloon out through the opening.

5. Next, push a new deflated balloon into the opening. This time, have your adult partner blow to fully inflate the balloon. As the balloon swells bigger, the papier-mâché will split open.

6. Once this happens, tie a knot in the neck of the balloon. Then gently tug out the balloon.

INDEX

PHOTO ACKNOWLEDGMENTS

The images in this book are used with the permission of: © Mark Moffett/Minden Pictures,
pp. 4, 8, 18–19; © Wegner/ARCO/naturepl.com, p. 5; © Rick C. West, pp. 6, 9 (top), 20–21, 22, 26,
27, 36, 47; © Steve Cooper/Photo Researchers, Inc., p. 7; © Andrew Syred/Photo Researchers,
Inc., p. 7 (inset); © Daniel Heuclin/NHPA/Photoshot, pp. 9 (bottom), 37, 41 (top); © Joel
Sartore/National Geographic Stock, pp. 10–11; © Laura Westlund/Independent Picture Service,
pp. 12–13; © Kenneth M. Highfill/Photo Researchers, Inc., p. 15; © Francesco Tomasinelli
& Emanuele Biggi/Photo Researchers, Inc., p. 17; © Stephen Dalton/Minden Pictures, p. 23;
© Austin J. Stevens/Animals Animals, p. 24; © Dante Fenolio/Photo Researchers, Inc., p. 25;
© Francesco Tomasinelli/Photo Researchers, Inc., p. 29; © Simon D. Pollard/Photo Researchers,
Inc., pp. 30, 31; © Francesco Tomasinelli/Natural Visions, pp. 33, 34–35; © Jany Sauvanet/Photo
Researchers, Inc., p. 39; © Martin Withers/Minden Pictures, p. 41 (bottom).

Front cover: © Rich Reid/National Geographic/Getty Images.

Main body text set in Glypha LT Std 55 Roman 12/20. Typeface provided by Adobe Systems.